BEAT THE CLOCK

Photography by
Scott Morrison

Written by
Moira Butterfield

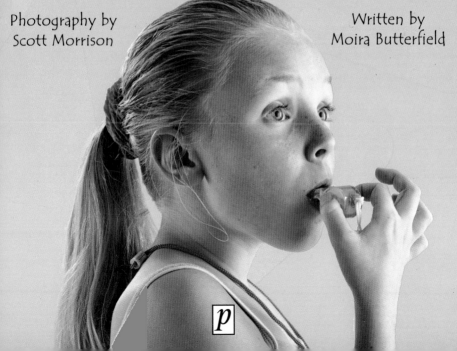

This is a Parragon book
First published in 2005
Parragon, Queen Street House, 4 Queen Street
Bath, BA1 1HE, UK
Copyright © Parragon 2005

Designed by Starry Dog Books Ltd.

ISBN 1-40545-382-6
Printed in China

CONTENTS

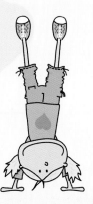

TIMING IT YOUR WAY
Children have tested all the games in this book to help us suggest times and distances. Everyone is different, though,so feel free to choose the best times and distances for yourself.

WARMING UP
Before you try athletic exercises, warm up your muscles first. Stretch out your arms and lift your knees a few times. You are likely to be quicker if you warm up like this.

> **TIMING TIP**
> *You can improve your times
> by practising. Keep a note
> of your results and try
> to beat them!*

THE WINNER!
Give out medals,
stickers and certificates
to game winners.

STOPWATCH PARTY
This pack has everything you
need for a stopwatch
sleepover or party. Before
the party starts, make a list
of games you want to
try and gather together
the things you'll need.

5

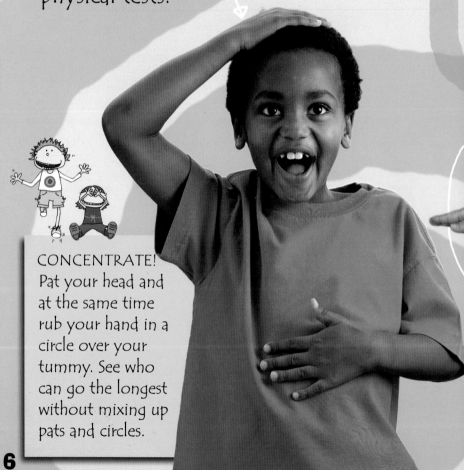

GET MOVING!
Take it in turns to time you and your friends doing these indoor physical tests.

CONCENTRATE!
Pat your head and at the same time rub your hand in a circle over your tummy. See who can go the longest without mixing up pats and circles.

WHEN WILL YOU CRACK?

Kneel on the floor, staring at the person holding the stopwatch. How long will it be before you blink?

CAN YOU STAND IT?

Stand on one leg. Grab hold of your other foot and hold it behind your knee. Then shut your eyes. Who balances for the longest?

STRONG-ARM STRETCH

Stretch your arms out sideways and hold them up level with your shoulders. Move them in little circles. Who will last the longest in this tough test of arm strength?

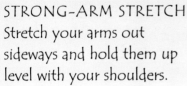

7

INDOOR OLYMPICS

FLOOR FUN
Here are two funny floor games to play using your stopwatch.

ROLLABALL
1. Set up a course on the floor, lining up small objects about 50cm apart.

2. Take it in turns to blow the ball along the course, weaving round the objects. Blow the ball to one end and then back.

The winner is the player who completes the course in the fastest time.

You need:
Newspaper or tissue paper scrunched into a ball.
Drinking straws.
Small objects such as sweets.
Tape measure.
Two books to mark either end of your course.

Stopwatch fun for indoor days

FISHFACE RACE

You need:
Sheets of newspaper.
Scissors and a ruler.
Drinking straws and a tape measure.
Two books to mark either
end of your course.

1. Get each player to cut a fish shape out of newspaper, roughly 17cm long and 8cm across its widest part. Give each player a straw and set up a course about 2m long.

2. Suck up the fish with the straw and carry it along. If you drop it, suck it up again.

3 Take it in turns to go to the end of the course and back again. The winner is the one who is fastest.

TABLETOP TIMING
These indoor time trials are designed for you to do on a tabletop.

You need:
One big tiddlywink and lots of little tiddlywinks.
A small saucer and a ruler.

TIDDLYWINK TIMING
1 Put a pile of tiddlywinks about 20cm away from the saucer.

2 Use the big tiddlywink to flick the others into the saucer. How many can you flick into the plate in one minute?

TIDDLYWINK TIP
TIDDLYWINKS WORK WELL WHEN PLAYED ON THE CARPET.

RAISIN' RAISINS

Start with a pile of raisins, a plate and a straw. How many raisins can you suck up with the straw and transfer to the plate in one minute?

TABLETOP BUILDING

Stack dominos, one on top of the other.

How high can you make your stack in 15 seconds?

11

INDOOR OLYMPICS

TEAM TIMING
These timed games are great for parties and sleepovers.

BALLOONARAMA

You need:
Party balloons.
Tape measure.
Objects to mark the start and finish.

1 Take it in turns to hop along a course 500cm long (to measure this roughly put one foot in front of the other 25 times).

2 Carry a balloon between your knees. You can pick it up if it falls. Time yourself to the far end and back.

BUCKET CHUCKIT

You need:
A bucket.
A big bag of wrapped chewy
sweets, or some bean bags.
A tape measure.

GAMES TIP
ADD TO THE GAME
FUN BY PLAYING SOME
FAST MUSIC IN THE
BACKGROUND!

1 Stand about 80cm
away from the bucket.
How many sweets can
you throw into the
bucket in one minute?

OUTDOOR OLYMPICS

SUPERFAST RUNNING
A stopwatch can help you get fit. You will do better at outdoor games and look healthier, too!

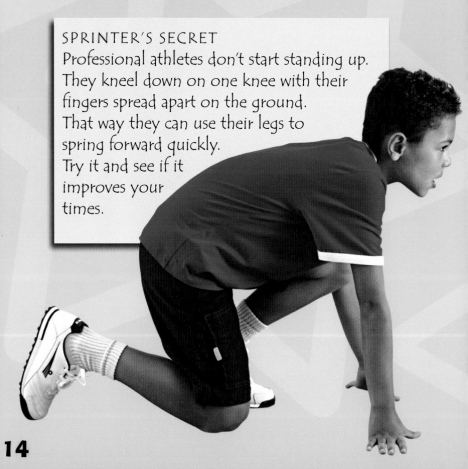

SPRINTER'S SECRET
Professional athletes don't start standing up. They kneel down on one knee with their fingers spread apart on the ground. That way they can use their legs to spring forward quickly. Try it and see if it improves your times.

RUNNING CHAMPION

Choose a long track such as round a playing field, or a short track such as up and down a garden. Get a friend to time you, or carry the watch in your hand as you run along, to time yourself.

Run one lap of a playing field, or several laps up and down your garden, and write down your time. Then try to improve on it. Keep a note of your times and the dates you did them.

RUNNING TIP
YOU'LL FIND YOU GET FASTER THE MORE YOU PRACTISE.

ASSAULT COURSE ACTION

Here are some ideas for setting up an
outdoor assault course. Clearly mark a
'start' and 'finish' line and set up the
obstacles in between. Time your
progress from start to finish,
holding the watch yourself or
getting a friend to help. If it's a
short course, go round twice.

SWEETIE STOP

Mark a point about
80cm away from a
bucket, and hand each runner a wrapped
sweet. On the way round runners must
stop at this mark and throw a sweet into
the bucket, before carrying on.

LEAP ALONG
Lay out five or six small objects about 15cm apart in a line. Apples, plastic flowerpots, fist-sized garden stones or bean bags will all do. Runners must leap between each object.

DECKCHAIR HOP
Add a deckchair to your course. Runners must hop right around the chair before they carry on.

WORK WITH WHAT YOU'VE GOT
You could plan your assault course round objects that are already outside, such as trees, posts or paths. Tell runners to run round a tree a couple of times or jump over a path.

OUTDOOR OLYMPICS

MINUTE CHALLENGE
How many of these can you do in one minute?

MINI LAPS
Run to and fro between two markers about 775cm apart (measure it roughly by putting one foot in front of the other 40 times).

STAR JUMPS
Jump up in the air, spreading out your arms and legs. Count out loud as you jump.

MINI HOP LAPS
Hop to and fro
between two markers.
Count your laps as
you complete them.

BACK HOPS
Try hopping your
laps backwards.
It's harder than
you think!

*LAP TIP
IF YOU LIKE,
ADD OBJECTS
SUCH AS
APPLES
BETWEEN THE
MARKERS.
WEAVE
ROUND THEM
AS YOU RUN
OR HOP.*

19

WET AND WILD
Here is a funny outdoor game to play with your friends and your stopwatch.

You need:
A plastic or paper picnic cup.
A bowl of water, a table and a bucket.
A dry stick for each player.
A pencil.
A towel to dry off afterwards.

1 Measure out a course roughly 775cm long
(see p18). Put the bowl of water on a picnic
table at the start of the course. Stand the bucket
at the finish point.

2 Start the watch. The first player must fill the
cup with water from the bowl and carry it
between their teeth to the bucket. They must
empty the water into the bucket without using
their hands or dropping the cup.

3 They must run back with
the cup between their teeth
and do it all over again, until
one minute is up.

Use the stick to measure the height of the
water in the bucket. Mark the height on the
stick. The winner is the player who achieves the
highest water level after one minute.

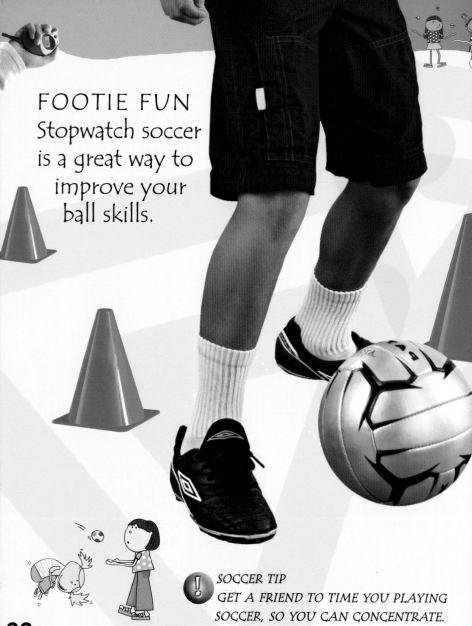

FOOTIE FUN
Stopwatch soccer is a great way to improve your ball skills.

SOCCER TIP
GET A FRIEND TO TIME YOU PLAYING
SOCCER, SO YOU CAN CONCENTRATE.

MINUTE SCORER

How many times can you score against a goalkeeper in one minute? Stand 500cm from the goalie (that's roughly one foot in front of the other 25 times). You must collect the ball yourself after each attempt.

DRIBBLING COURSE

Set up a course using cones or objects such as apples or bean bags. Dribble the ball from one end to the other, in an s-shape round the obstacles. Time how long it takes you to go one way and then back the other. Remember, you must dribble round every object for your run to count!

BALL ACTION

Here are some games to try with a basketball or mini bouncing balls.

STOPWATCH BASKETBALL

How many times can you shoot a basketball into a net in one minute? Stand about 240cm away from it (roughly 12 small steps). After each try, collect your ball and run back to shoot again.

JUST A JUGGLING MINUTE!

See how long you can juggle two small balls or a couple of oranges. If juggling is too hard, throw the balls between you and a friend and see how long you can keep going before you drop one.

BOUNCY BOUNCY

How long can you bounce a ball up and down, before it rolls away from you?

25

WORDS, WORDS, WORDS
Get out your pencils and paper for these timed team word games.

SPEED POETRY
You have two minutes to write a poem. When the time is up, read out your masterpiece!

ALPHABET RACE

You have two minutes to write a list of objects, each one beginning with a different letter of the alphabet. The winner is the one who gets furthest through the alphabet in one minute. After the time is up, take it in turns to read your list out.

WORD SEARCH

Decide between you on a group of letters - you need four vowels (a, e, i, o or u) and 8 other letters. Then give yourselves two minutes to make as many words as you can from the letter list. The winner is the player with the most words once the time is up.

LETTER LIST

How many things beginning with A can you write down or say out loud in one minute? Once you have done A, try each letter of the alphabet. Keep a score for each letter. The winner is the one with the highest score.

TIME TIP

EXPERIMENT AND CHOOSE YOUR OWN TIMES FOR THESE CHALLENGES. SOME OF YOU MAY BE SLOW WRITERS. IT DOESN'T MEAN YOU'RE NOT BRAINBOXES!

BRAINBOX CHALLENGE

CAR OLYMPICS
These stopwatch games are for playing on car journeys.

GUESS THE TIME
Ask a friend to start the watch. Then try to guess when a minute is up. Take it in turns to see who guesses the closest.

BLUE TRUCK
Start the watch and time how long it takes you to spot a blue truck. You could take guesses beforehand on how long it will take, and see whose guess is closest. Try spotting other objects, too, such as a yellow car or a motorbike.

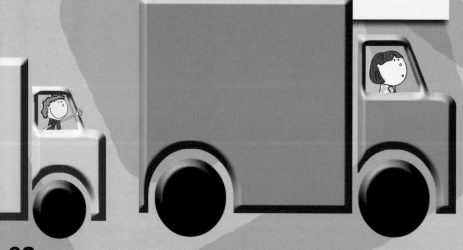

A stopwatch brain workout

YES, NO
Start the watch. Then ask a player questions, trying to get them to say "yes" or "no". Time how long they can last before they slip up. The faster you ask the questions, the more likely it is you'll catch them out.

GUESS THE JOURNEY TIME
On short trips, guess how long the journey is going to take beforehand. Then time it to find out who guessed closest.

BRAINBOX CHALLENGE

ART OLYMPICS
Here are some timed games that will bring out the artistic genius in you!

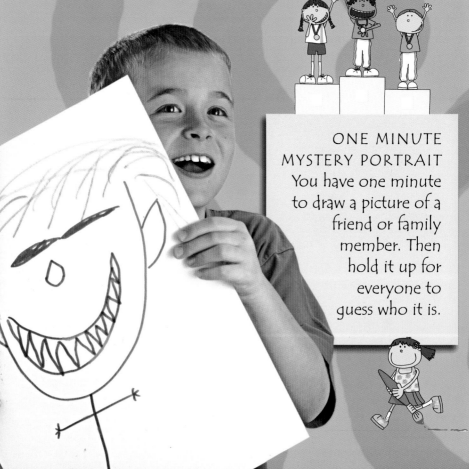

ONE MINUTE MYSTERY PORTRAIT
You have one minute to draw a picture of a friend or family member. Then hold it up for everyone to guess who it is.

A stopwatch brain workout

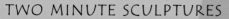

TWO MINUTE SCULPTURES
Give yourselves two minutes to make models from plasticine. If you like, add pipecleaners and drinking straws, too. When the time is up, get your friends to guess what you have made.

ONE-MINUTE SELF-PORTRAIT
You have one minute to draw your self-portrait. Then hold it up for everyone to see!

REMEMBER, REMEMBER
This classic 'memory tray' game is ideal for a party or a sleepover.

You need:
A drinks tray.
A teatowel.
A collection of
10 everyday objects.

Arrange the objects on the tray. Cover it with a teatowel and put it in front of your friends. Whip off the teatowel for 30 seconds; then take the tray away and give players a minute to write down what they can remember. The winner is the one who remembers the most.